SKILLS PRACTICE

Volume 1

PEARSON

Copyright © 2009 by Pearson Education, Inc. or its affiliate(s). All rights reserved. Printed in the United States of America. This publication is protected by copyright, and permission should be obtained from the publisher prior to any prohibited reproductions, storage in a retrieval system, or transmission in any form or by any means, electronic, mechanical, photocopying, recording, or likewise. For information regarding permission(s), write to: Pearson School Rights & Permissions Department, One Lake Street, Upper Saddle River, New Jersey 07458.

Pearson® is a trademark, in the U.S. and/or in other countries, of Pearson Education, Inc. or its affiliate(s).

ISBN 13: 978-0-7854-6621-5
ISBN 10:   0-7854-6621-5
2 3 4 5 6 7 8 9 10   V016   12 11 10 09

1-800-992-0244
www.pearson.com

CONTENTS

Unit 2, Lesson 1: Ratios and Proportionality

Solve for *n*.

1. $\frac{3}{6} = \frac{n}{12}$ _____

2. $\frac{2}{7} = \frac{16}{n}$ _____

3. $\frac{10}{n} = \frac{30}{12}$ _____

4. $\frac{n}{9} = \frac{9}{81}$ _____

5. $\frac{5}{n} = \frac{20}{32}$ _____

6. $\frac{1}{4} = \frac{n}{36}$ _____

7. $\frac{6}{12} = \frac{24}{n}$ _____

8. $\frac{7}{8} = \frac{35}{n}$ _____

9. $\frac{4}{11} = \frac{n}{33}$ _____

10. $\frac{n}{20} = \frac{15}{100}$ _____

11. $\frac{9}{21} = \frac{3}{n}$ _____

12. $\frac{2}{7} = \frac{n}{56}$ _____

13. $\frac{6}{9} = \frac{n}{36}$ _____

14. $\frac{3}{5} = \frac{n}{25}$ _____

15. $\frac{12}{2} = \frac{n}{6}$ _____

16. $\frac{12}{15} = \frac{n}{5}$ _____

17. $\frac{40}{80} = \frac{n}{4}$ _____

18. $\frac{1}{2} = \frac{n}{36}$ _____

19. $\frac{8}{12} = \frac{n}{9}$ _____

20. $\frac{2}{3} = \frac{n}{30}$ _____

Solve.

21. Sally delivers 5 newspapers every 15 minutes. At the same rate, how many newspapers can she deliver in 45 minutes?
_____

22. The movie rental special is 2 for $7.50. Joe has $23. How many movies can he rent? _____

23. Kate cuts 6 carrots into three bowls of salad. What would be the ratio of carrots per salad? _____

24. A bag filled with red marbles and blue marbles has a ratio of 2:3. If there are 18 blue marbles, how many are red?
_____

Unit 2, Lesson 1: Ratios and Proportionality

Complete the table below by solving for the missing variable, when xy = 100.

	x	y
1.	_____	100
2.	2	_____
3.	_____	5
4.	4	_____
5.	10	_____

Complete the table below by solving for the missing variable, when $\frac{2}{6} = \frac{x}{y}$.

	x	y
6.	4	_____
7.	_____	30
8.	9	_____
9.	_____	33
10.	3	_____

Solve.

11. Terra can swim 12 laps every 30 minutes. How many laps can Terra swim in 220 minutes? _____

12. Out of 30 radio stations, 14 are playing commercials at 3:00 PM Write this as a ratio in simplest form. _____

Unit 2, Lesson 3: Proportionality and Percents

Find each answer.

1. 15% of 20

_____

2. 40% of 80

_____

3. 20% of 45

_____

4. 18% of 70

_____

5. 90% of 120

_____

6. 65% of 700

_____

7. 25% of 84

_____

8. 63% of 80

_____

9. 60% of 50

_____

10. 45% of 90

_____

11. 12% of 94

_____

12. 15% of 52

_____

13. 37% of 80

_____

14. 25% of 16

_____

15. 63% of 800

_____

16. 72% of 950

_____

17. 55% of 250

_____

18. 18% of 420

_____

19. 33% of 140

_____

20. 53% of 400

_____

Solve.

21. Teri used 60% of 20 gallons of paint. How much did she use?
_____

22. The Badgers won 75% of their 32 games this year. How many games did they win? _____

23. Vivian earned $540 last month. She saved 30% of this money. How much did she save? _____

24. A survey of the students at Lakeside School yielded the results shown in the table at the right. There are 1,400 students enrolled at Lakeside. Complete the table for the number of students in each activity.

How Lakeside Students Spend Their Time on Saturday		
Activity	**Percent of Students**	**Number of Students**
Babysitting	22%	
Sports	26%	
Job	15%	
At home	10%	
Tutoring	10%	
Other	17%	

Unit 2, Lesson 3: Proportionality and Percents

Find each answer.

1. 25% of 100

_____

2. 70% of 70

_____

3. 10% of 70

_____

4. 75% of 40

_____

5. 80% of 50

_____

6. 12% of 60

_____

7. 24% of 80

_____

8. 45% of 90

_____

9. 60% of 72

_____

10. 55% of 120

_____

11. 95% of 180

_____

12. 16% of 80

_____

Solve using the table.

13. What percent of the 40 girls preferred the Prime Numbers? _____

14. What percent of the 40 girls were undecided? _____

15. Which group was the most popular? _____

Favorite Music Groups (40 girls surveyed)	
Prime Numbers	12 girls
Acute Angles	$\frac{1}{4}$ of the girls
Square Roots	35% of the girls
Undecided	4 girls

Circle the correct answer.

16. 9 is what percent of 20?

   A 22.2%   **C** 222%

   B 45%   **D** 4.5%

17. Find 60% of 92.

   A $153\frac{1}{3}$ **C** 552

   B 5.52   **D** 55.2

Unit 2, Lesson 6:
Solving Problems with Proportionality

Fill out the chart below. Find the discount amount for each item. Then find the sale price.

Discount Rate	Price of Item	Discount Amount	Sale Price
1. 6%	$18	_____	_____
2. 22%	$213	_____	_____
3. 18%	$80	_____	_____
4. 9%	$124	_____	_____
5. 42%	$672	_____	_____

Solve.

6. A savings account has $456. The bank offers 3% interest per year on accounts. How much interest would this account earn in one year? _____

7. Laney buys a movie for $12.99. The movie has a sales tax of 7%. What is the total cost of the movie, including tax? _____

8. A hat Juan wants costs $30. Today, the hat is discounted 15%. Juan has $27. Can he buy the hat? _____

9. Bicycles are discounted 30%. How much will a $180 bike cost after the discount? _____

10. A bank is offering a 5% annual interest rate. How much interest would $48 make in one year? _____

Unit 2, Lesson 6:
Solving Problems with Proportionality

You are at a restaurant and want to tip the waitress 20%. Find the total cost of each meal choice, with the tip included, to fill in the chart.

Menu Item	Price	Total Cost (with tip)
1. Hamburger	$7.50	_____
2. Tacos	$12	_____
3. Spaghetti	$15	_____
4. Pizza (slice)	$1.50	_____
5. Pie	$4	_____
6. Steak	$35	_____
7. Soda	$2.50	_____

Solve.

8. Anedra is buying a car that costs $12,500. Sales tax on the car is 7%. What is the total cost of the car? _____

9. The car dealer offers Anedra 3% off the total cost of the car. How much will she owe after the discount? _____

10. Anedra also needs to buy new license tabs for her car. The tabs cost $120, plus an 8% tax. How much do the tabs cost with tax? _____

Name _____   Date _____

Unit 2, Lesson 9:
Proportions, Predictions, and Probability

Make a prediction for each.

1. Tanya is flipping through TV channels. She notices that
   12 of the 50 channels are showing commercials.
   How many channels would be showing commercials
   if she had 250 channels? _____

2. At a concert hall, 3 out of every 100 shows are cancelled.
   If 600 shows are scheduled, how many will be cancelled?

   _____

3. Each month, Matt drives by the Pine Street stoplight 20 times.
   Last month it was green 6 times, yellow 4 times, and red 10
   times. In the next 12 months, how many times will the light
   be red? _____

4. In the next 12 months, how many times will the light be green?

   _____

5. In the next 12 months, how many times will the light be yellow?

   _____

Solve for x.

6. $\frac{2}{4} = \frac{x}{12}$ _____

7. $\frac{1.2}{7.5} = \frac{3}{x}$ _____

8. $\frac{5}{6} = \frac{45}{x}$ _____

9. $\frac{10}{1} = \frac{x}{7}$ _____

10. $\frac{6.2}{x} = \frac{8}{20}$ _____

Unit 2, Lesson 9:
Proportions, Predictions, and Probability

Use the tally chart for questions 1–7.

1. For science class, Kendra was experimenting how many times she would roll a certain number from the die. How many times total did Kendra roll the die?

   _____

Die Number	Times Rolled
1	ЖЖ ЖЖ
2	ЖЖ I
3	III
4	ЖЖ II
5	II
6	ЖЖ ЖЖ II

2. Using her results, predict how many times a six would be picked during 120 rolls. _____

3. Using her results, predict how many times a three would be picked during 120 rolls. _____

4. Using her results, predict how many times a two would be picked during 120 rolls. _____

5. If Kendra rolled the die 320 times, how many fives would she roll? _____

6. What percentage of Kendra's rolls resulted in a one or a six? _____

7. What percentage of Kendra's rolls resulted in a 2 or a 4? _____

Solve for x.

8. $\frac{14}{28} = \frac{x}{8}$ _____

9. $\frac{5.5}{55} = \frac{1}{x}$ _____

10. $\frac{18}{x} = \frac{3}{4}$ _____

Name _____ Date _____

Unit 2, Lesson 11:
Similar Figures and Scale Factors

Find the scale factor of the smaller figure to the larger figure. Simplify when possible.

1.

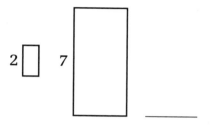

2   7

_____

5.

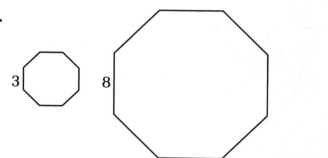

3   8

_____

2.

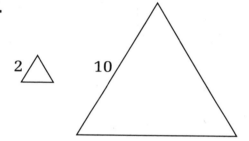

2   10

_____

6.

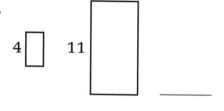

4   11

_____

3.

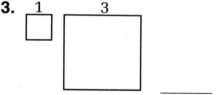

1   3

_____

7.

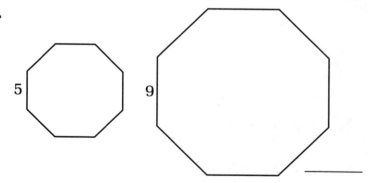

5   9

_____

4.

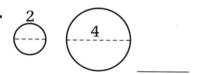

2   4

_____

8.

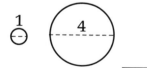

1   4

_____

Unit 2, Lesson 11:
Similar Figures and Scale Factors

Determine if the figures below are similar. Write *yes* or *no*.

1.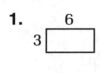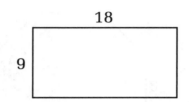

6   18

3   9

_____

3.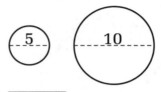

5   10

_____

2.

4   8

4   3

_____

4.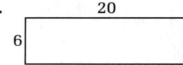

20   15

6   7

_____

Find the length of the missing side using the listed scale factor.

5. Scale factor = 1:2.5

4

?

_____

7. Scale factor = 1:3

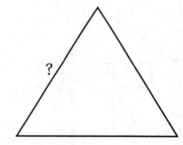

11

?

_____

6. Scale factor = 4:1

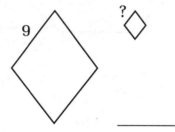

9

?

_____

8. Scale factor = 2:1

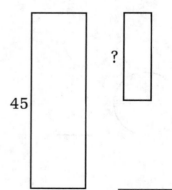

45

?

_____

Name _____ Date _____

Unit 2, Lesson 13: Proportionality and Graphing

Determine the rate of each.

1. A large pizza with 12 slices costs $22. What is the cost per slice? _____

2. Six containers of bottled water cost $2.40. What is the cost per bottle? _____

3. A person bikes 16.6 miles in 4 hours. What is the rate per hour? _____

4. One dozen eggs cost $1.80. What is the cost per egg? _____

5. T-shirts are two for $17.50. What is the cost per shirt? _____

6. You are paid $86 for working 8 hours. What is the rate per hour? _____

7. You swim 6.5 miles in 2 hours. What is the rate per hour? _____

8. You send 50 text messages for $5.00. What is the cost per message? _____

9. Forty pounds of dog food costs $25. What is the cost per pound? _____

10. You drive 220 miles in 4 hours. What is the rate per hour? _____

Find the slope of the line through each pair of points.

11. (3, 3) (4, 6) _____

12. (4, 2) (8, 7) _____

13. (1, 3) (10, 5) _____

14. (7, 8) (15, 9) _____

15. (5, 5) (14, 6) _____

Unit 2, Lesson 13: Proportionality and Graphing

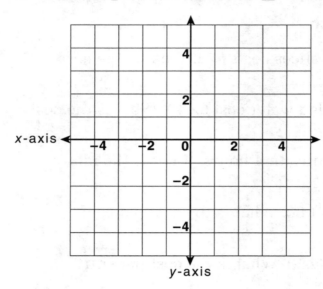

Plot the following points on the graph.

1. (3, 0)

2. (2, 4)

3. (1, −4)

4. (−1, 2)

5. (−2, −3)

6. (−4, 4)

Name _____ Date _____

Unit 2, Lesson 16:
Percentages, Histograms, and Circle Graphs

Find the percentage or number.

1. What is 33% of 602? _____

2. 8 is what percent of 20? _____

3. 12 is what percent of 500? _____

4. What is 7% of 110? _____

5. What is 85% of 25? _____

6. 91 is 10% of what number? _____

7. 87 is what percent of 120? _____

8. What is 45% of 800? _____

9. What is 2% of 60? _____

10. What is 15% of 303? _____

Decide whether the information should be shown on a circle graph or a histogram.

11. favorite food of everyone in your class _____

12. your change in height each year _____

13. company profits and losses for one year _____

14. type of car 100 different people own _____

15. eye color of everyone in your family _____

Unit 2, Lesson 16:
Percentages, Histograms, and Circle Graphs

Use the circle graph to answer questions 1–5. The circle graph includes data from a survey of 200 people.

1. How many people said green is their favorite color? _____

2. How many people did not pick blue, red, or green as their favorite color? _____

3. How many people picked blue or red as their favorite color? _____

4. If 800 people were surveyed instead of 200 people, how many would pick a color other than red, blue, or green as their favorite color? _____

5. If 50 people were surveyed instead of 200 people, how many would pick red as their favorite color? _____

Favorite Color

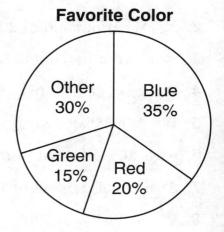

Find the percentage.

6. 15 people are surveyed. 9 choose comedy as their favorite type of movie. _____

7. 300 people are surveyed. 288 wear a watch. _____

8. 43 people are surveyed. 4 own a snowboard. _____

9. 500 people are surveyed. 356 own more than 10 pairs of shoes. _____

10. 82 people are surveyed. 24 play an instrument. _____

11. 125 people are surveyed. 60 choose cherry as their favorite pie. _____

12. 65 people are surveyed. 2 do not own a computer. _____

Unit 2, Lesson 19: Populations and Samples

Predict the number of people responding "yes" given the survey information and total population.

1. 100 surveyed
25 say yes
total population = 600

_____

2. 50 surveyed
5 say yes
total population = 80

_____

3. 8 surveyed
2 say yes
total population = 12

_____

4. 25 surveyed
21 say yes
total population = 300

_____

5. 200 surveyed
60 say yes
total population = 3,000

_____

Predict the number of people responding "no" given the survey information and total population.

6. 400 surveyed
130 say no
total population = 1,600

_____

7. 225 surveyed
18 say no
total population = 5,000

_____

8. 75 surveyed
30 say no
total population = 150

_____

9. 800 surveyed
640 say no
total population = 12,000

_____

10. 60 surveyed
3 say no
total population = 100

_____

Solve.

11. At the fair on Thursday, 30 people out of 100 ride on the ferris wheel. On Friday, 250 people are at the fair. Predict how many will ride the ferris wheel. _____

12. In your neighborhood, 4 out of 20 households water their lawn every Tuesday. If your city has 2,500 households, how many water their lawn on Tuesdays? _____

Unit 2, Lesson 19: Populations and Samples

Use the bar graph to answer questions 1–5. Fifty people are at the grocery store. The total town population is 2,000.

1. Based on the total population, how many people buy fruit? _____

2. Based on the total population, how many people buy cereal? How many do not buy cereal? _____

3. Based on the total population, how many people buy soup? _____

4. If the total population were 40,000, how many people would buy meat?
   _____

5. If the total population were 800, how many people would buy eggs? _____

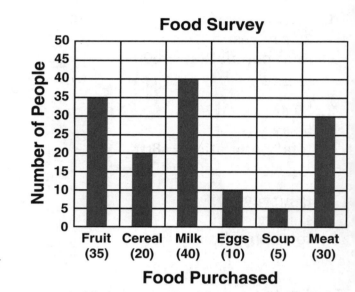

Food Survey

Number of People

50
45
40
35
30
25
20
15
10
5
0

Fruit (35) Cereal (20) Milk (40) Eggs (10) Soup (5) Meat (30)

Food Purchased

Unit 3, Lesson 1: Integers and Rational Numbers

Find the absolute value of each number.

1. |56| _____

2. |−14| _____

3. |4,312| _____

4. |−218| _____

5. |−111| _____

6. |3,529| _____

7. |−5| _____

8. |−78| _____

Write the opposite integer.

9. −1 _____

10. 756 _____

11. 9,023 _____

12. −61 _____

13. −26 _____

14. 813 _____

Use > or < to compare.

15. −3 _____ 3

16. −17 _____ 21

17. 38 _____ −380

18. 0 _____ −2

19. −10 _____ −20

20. 0 _____ 3

Unit 3, Lesson 1: Integers and Rational Numbers

Put the integers in order from greatest to least.

1. −22, 18, −9, 4, −1 _____

2. 0, −5, 1, −1, 10 _____

3. −32, −64, −11, 3, −10 _____

4. 19, 0, 82, −19, −2 _____

5. 1, −77, −100, 12, −6 _____

Find a rational number between the two given numbers.

6. 4.5 _____ 4.8

7. $6\frac{1}{2}$ _____ 7

8. 9 _____ $10\frac{1}{2}$

9. 16.5 _____ 17

10. $\frac{6}{8}$ _____ $\frac{10}{8}$

List the integer that describes each situation.

11. Decrease of 3 pounds _____

12. Gain of 12 points _____

13. Withdrawal of $187 _____

14. Reduction of 56 buses _____

15. Addition of 8 puppies _____

16. Rise of 24 degrees in temperature _____

Unit 3, Lesson 3:
Adding and Subtracting Negative Numbers

Find the sum or difference.

1. $-7 + 36 =$ _____

2. $-3 - 82 =$ _____

3. $-27 + (-10) =$ _____

4. $-6 + 143 =$ _____

5. $-303 + 510 =$ _____

6. $-40 - 11 =$ _____

7. $-25 + 25 =$ _____

8. $-74 - (-15) =$ _____

9. $-320 + (-8) =$ _____

10. $9 + (-5) =$ _____

11. $(-27 + 4) - 10 =$ _____

12. $-3 + 3 =$ _____

13. $(90 + 7) - (212 + -52) =$ _____

14. $(-18 - 17) + (-81 + 15) =$ _____

15. $0 + (-62 + 19) - 71 =$ _____

Match each expression with the correct answer.

16. $-58 - (-23) =$ _____   **A** 407

17. $-150 + 150 =$ _____   **B** 0

18. $11 + (-96 - 39) + 2 =$ _____   **C** -122

19. $-350 + 820 + (-63) =$ _____   **D** -7

20. $(10 - 7) + -10 =$ _____   **E** -35

Unit 3, Lesson 3:
Adding and Subtracting Negative Numbers

Write the additive inverse of each number.

1. −512 _____

2. 105 _____

3. 7 _____

On a separate sheet of paper, draw a number line to solve.

4. −3 + 6 = _____

5. −5 + (−4) = _____

6. 0 − 5 = _____

7. −1 + 3 = _____

8. −3 + (−2) + (−4) = _____

Solve. Show your work.

9. Olivia is working on a science project about temperatures. Some of the temperatures that she has recorded over the last six months include: 25, −13, −9, 62, 47, and −2. If Olivia added all of these temperatures together, what number would she get?

_____

10. What number would Olivia get if she subtracted all of the numbers from question 9?

_____

11. During Andrew's football game, his team lost 12 yards, lost 3 yards, gained 7 yards, gained 14 yards, and lost 9 yards. Add all the numbers together to find out the total number of yards that Andrew's team gained or lost.

_____

12. Jasmine owes her friend $18. She pays him back $5. Then Jasmine needs to borrow $10 more. A few days later she pays him back $7. How much does Jasmine still owe her friend?

_____

Unit 3, Lesson 6:
Multiplying and Dividing Negative Numbers

Find each product or quotient.

1. $14 \times -8 = $ _____

2. $-5 \times -11 = $ _____

3. $-150 \div (-30) = $ _____

4. $86 \div (-2) = $ _____

5. $-220 \div (-10) = $ _____

6. $56 \div (-4) = $ _____

7. $-23 \times 8 = $ _____

8. $-620 \div (-5) = $ _____

9. $36 \times -23 = $ _____

10. $-47 \times -4 = $ _____

11. $-800 \div 50 = $ _____

12. $2{,}022 \times -1 = $ _____

13. $9{,}300 \div (-60) = $ _____

14. $-8 \times -3 \times -2 \times -7 = $ _____

Unit 3, Lesson 6:
Multiplying and Dividing Negative Numbers

Match each expression with the correct answer.

1. $-740 \div 20 =$ _____

2. $-63 \times (-11) =$ _____

3. $-85 \times 7 =$ _____

4. $63 \div (-3) =$ _____

5. $-26 \times 5 =$ _____

6. $71 \times (-3) =$ _____

7. $-48 \div (-24) =$ _____

8. $39 \times (-12) =$ _____

A -21

B 595

C -130

D 2

E -37

F -693

G 130

H -468

I 693

J 37

K -213

L -595

Circle the correct answer.

9. When multiplying or dividing two negative numbers, the answer will be:

              negative   positive

10. $-88 \div (-4) =$

              22   -22

11. When multiplying or dividing one negative number and one positive number, the answer will be:

              negative   positive

12. $-22 \times 7 =$

    154   -154 145 -145

Unit 3, Lesson 9: Formulas with Fractions

Solve for x. Put your answer in simplest form. Show your work.

1. $\frac{5}{6} = \frac{1}{4}x$ _____

5. $\frac{1}{5}x = \frac{7}{8}$ _____

2. $\frac{3}{4}x = \frac{2}{9}$ _____

6. $\frac{3}{7}x = \frac{8}{15}$ _____

3. $\frac{2}{3}x = \frac{6}{11}$ _____

7. $4\frac{1}{2}x = 9\frac{2}{5}$ _____

4. $\frac{4}{9} = \frac{2}{3}x$ _____

8. $6\frac{4}{5} = \frac{10}{7}x$ _____

Multiply both sides of the equation by the common denominator to solve. Put your answer in simplest form.

9. $\frac{1}{3}x = \frac{5}{9}$ _____

12. $\frac{1}{4}x = \frac{5}{9}$ _____

10. $\frac{3}{14} = \frac{2}{7}x$ _____

13. $\frac{2}{5} = \frac{2}{3}x$ _____

11. $\frac{4}{25}x = \frac{1}{5}$ _____

14. $\frac{3}{20}x = \frac{9}{10}$ _____

Unit 3, Lesson 9: Formulas with Fractions

Solve for x. Put your answer in simplest form.

1. $\frac{11}{40}x = \frac{3}{10}$ $x =$ _____

2. $\frac{5}{8} = \frac{3}{7}x$ $x =$ _____

3. $\frac{7}{12}x = \frac{8}{18}$ $x =$ _____

4. $\frac{3}{19}x = \frac{2}{5}$ $x =$ _____

5. $\frac{13}{21} = \frac{6}{7}x$ $x =$ _____

6. $\frac{11}{24}x = \frac{3}{8}$ $x =$ _____

7. $\frac{3}{16}x = \frac{2}{9}$ $x =$ _____

8. $\frac{5}{6}x = \frac{7}{24}$ $x =$ _____

9. $\frac{2}{11} = \frac{8}{33}x$ $x =$ _____

10. $\frac{5}{51}x = \frac{9}{10}$ $x =$ _____

11. $\frac{5}{6} = \frac{4}{54}x$ $x =$ _____

12. $\frac{2}{5}x = \frac{14}{75}$ $x =$ _____

Name _____   Date _____

Unit 3, Lesson 11:
Writing Linear Equations with Rational Numbers

Write the expression that represents each situation.

1. Yesenia lends 8 movies to a friend. She has 74 movies left.

   _____

2. Emma's hair is n inches long. Stacey's hair is 4 inches less than 2 times the length of Emma's hair. _____

3. Omari paid c dollars for a sweatshirt. Ted bought the same sweatshirt on sale one month later and paid half of what Omari paid. _____

4. William picks r apples a day for 4 days. By the end of the fourth day, William has 56 apples. _____

5. Together Dalia and William pick a total of 532 apples in 4 days. William picked 224 of the apples. How many apples did Dalia pick? _____

6. Carrie bakes 48 cookies. She gives each of her sisters one dozen cookies. How many sisters does Carrie have? _____

7. Essence makes $12 per hour. She works j hours. How much does she make? _____

8. June has 8 angel fish. She buys f fish. Now she has 17 fish.

   _____

9. Truen brings $600 with him for a vacation. He comes home from vacation with $180. How much did he spend? _____

10. Curt wins 4 wakeboarding competition trophies. Now he has a total of 12 trophies. How many trophies did Curt have before he won the 4 trophies? _____

11. Brooke has 15 pairs of shoes. She buys more shoes when they are on sale. Now she has a total of 23 pairs of shoes. How many pairs of shoes did Brooke buy on sale? _____

12. Mackenzie is buying turkey for a family meal. She guesses that each person will eat t pounds of turkey. If 8 people (including Mackenzie) are eating, how many pounds of turkey will Mackenzie need? _____

Writing Linear Equations with Rational Numbers   **29**

Name _____ Date _____

Unit 3, Lesson 11:
Writing Linear Equations with Rational Numbers

Write the inverse of each expression.

1. $j - 6 + 9$ _____

2. $\dfrac{400}{f}$ _____

3. $96 + c$ _____

4. $52x$ _____

5. $\dfrac{h}{84}$ _____

6. $k - 10 - 1$ _____

Write the expression that represents each situation.

7. Jeremy spends n dollars of his \$350 paycheck. _____

8. Natalie uses 200 cell phone minutes to talk an equal amount of time to n of her friends. _____

9. Allan drives 30 miles every day for n days. _____

10. Julie has 40 shirts, but she gives away n. _____

11. The water level n goes down 2 feet. _____

12. Karen puts 3 new cds in her cd collection n. _____

Unit 3, Lesson 13:
Solving Linear Equations with Rational Numbers

Solve for each variable.

1. $12 + j = 21$ _____

2. $y - 84 = 39$ _____

3. $s + 5 = -3$ _____

4. $31 = z + 12$ _____

5. $m - 2 = -7$ _____

6. $144 = n - 56$ _____

7. $90 + g = 42$ _____

8. $526 = 427 + p$ _____

9. $-72 + c = -72$ _____

10. $14 - k = 11$ _____

11. $88 = t - 27$ _____

12. $4 + g = 72$ _____

13. $105 = h + 18$ _____

14. $-32 = x + 10$ _____

15. $12x = 312$ _____

16. $\frac{60}{b} = 5$ _____

17. $\frac{e}{-15} = -14$ _____

18. $d(-5) = -400$ _____

19. $112 \times r = 896$ _____

20. $z + 22 = 6$ _____

Unit 3, Lesson 13:
Solving Linear Equations with Rational Numbers

Solve.

1. Ruby was washing dishes. It took her 2 minutes to wash and dry each dish. If dishes took Ruby 70 minutes to finish, how many dishes did she wash and dry? _____

2. Max is hungry and makes a sandwich. It takes him 4 minutes to make a sandwich. Next, Max makes a sandwich for his sister, mom, dad, and grandma. How long will it take Max to make all 4 sandwiches?

    _____

3. Tessa sells 6 of her horses. After the sale, she has only 9 horses left. How many horses did Tessa have before the sale? _____

4. Mia picks 8 pounds of apples at an apple orchard. The orchard charges $4 per pound of apples. How much does Mia owe for the apples she picked? _____

5. Caleb gets a paycheck for $126. He puts $90 into his savings account and the rest into his checking account. How much of Caleb's check went into his checking account? _____

6. Juan's cat, Tabby, weighs 20 pounds. Tabby has gained 6 pounds since her last vet visit. How much did Tabby used to weigh? _____

7. Devin drives 65 miles per hour. How many hours would it take him to get to his grandparents house that is 455 miles away? _____

8. Kiara makes 22 blankets. After selling some blankets, she has 9 blankets left. How many blankets did she sell?

    _____

Match each equation with the correct answer.

9. $\frac{52}{p} = 4$ _____   **A** $p = 85$

10. $9p = 135$ _____   **B** $p = 24$

11. $27 - 3 = p$ _____   **C** $p = 13$

12. $\frac{p}{17} = 5$ _____   **D** $p = 77$

13. $p + 12 = 89$ _____   **E** $p = 72$

14. $213 - p = 141$ _____   **F** $p = 15$

Name _____ Date _____

Unit 3, Lesson 16: Choosing the Best Procedures to Solve Linear Equations

Solve for _x_ to determine if the equations are equivalent. Write _yes_ or _no_.

1. $x + 2 = 21$ $5x + 10 = 105$ _____

2. $32x - 10 = 86$ $19x - 2 = 74$ _____

3. $6x = 96$ $0.75x = 12$ _____

4. $2x - 5 = 7$ $40x - 100 = 140$ _____

5. $32 + x = 35$ $256 + 8x = 280$ _____

6. $\frac{20}{x} = 5$ $\frac{104}{x} = 13$ _____

Solve for each variable. Show your work.

7. $8x + 15 = 79$ _____

8. $\frac{52}{s} + 10 = 14$ _____

9. $163 - d = 99$ _____

10. $4m = 212$ _____

11. $e + 303 = 450$ _____

12. $\frac{c}{24} - 7 = -12$ _____

Unit 3, Lesson 16: Choosing the Best Procedures to Solve Linear Equations

Solve for x to determine if the equations are equivalent. Write *yes* or *no*.

1. $4 + 8x = 108$ $8 + 16x = 216$ _____

2. $21p = 210$ $23p = 184$ _____

3. $25 + x = 61$ $40 + x = 76$ _____

4. $\frac{260}{t} = 130$ $\frac{3{,}120}{t} = 1{,}560$ _____

5. $g - 19 = 71$ $g - 36 = 49$ _____

Complete each sentence with the correct word.

    A equivalent   **B** both   **C** one   **D** not equivalent

6. Equations that have different solutions are _____.

7. The properties of equality state that numbers should be added, subtracted, divided, and multiplied by _____ side(s).

8. Equations that have the same solutions are _____.

Solve for each variable.

9. $35x = 420$ _____

10. $p - 74 = 540$ _____

11. $48n - (13 + 3) = 176$ _____

12. $63 = 3g$ _____

Name _____ Date _____

Unit 3, Lesson 19:
Prime Numbers and Prime Factorization

Find the prime factorization of each number by writing the appropriate numbers in the blanks.

1.

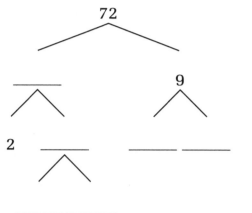

Prime factorization of 72: _____

2.

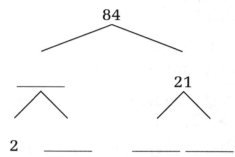

Prime factorization of 84: _____

Write the prime factorization.

3. 12 _____

4. 36 _____

5. 20 _____

6. 21 _____

7. 630 _____

8. 400 _____

9. 40 _____

10. 60 _____

11. 30 _____

12. 18 _____

13. 100 _____

14. 2,000 _____

15. 64 _____

16. 560 _____

Unit 3, Lesson 19:
Prime Numbers and Prime Factorization

Solve.

1. The prime factorization of a number is $2^3 \times 3^3 \times 5^3$. What is the number? _____

2. Could $2 \times 4 \times 5 \times 9 \times 11$ be the prime factorization of a number? Explain. _____

3. What number has a prime factorization of $2^3 \times 7$? _____

4. Holly says the prime factorization for 44 is 4×11. Is she right? Why or why not? _____

Circle the correct answer.

5. Which is the prime factorization of 48?

    A $2^4 \times 3$ **C** 4×12

    B $3^2 \times 6$ **D** 3×16

6. Which number is prime?

    F 62   **G** 77   **H** 95   **I** 53

Write the prime factorization of each number.

7. 45   8. 36   9. 42

If the number is prime, write *prime*. If the number is composite, write the prime factorization of the number.

10. 11 _____   13. 18 _____

11. 16 _____   14. 17 _____

12. 35 _____

Unit 4, Lesson 1: Linear Functions, Linear Equations, and Systems of Linear Equations

Complete the following statements using words from the box.

1. A linear equation has _____ variable(s).

2. $f(x) = 4 - 6x$ and $f(x) = 3x + 4$ are linear _____.

3. The _____ is the set of all values of y.

4. When graphed, a linear equation creates a _____ line.

5. The function of x can be represented by _____.

6. $5x + 4y = 13$ and $4x + 3y = 7$ are a(n) _____.

straight
one
functions
domain
expressions
linear
$f(x)$
two
different
systems
curved
system of linear equations
matching
$x(f)$
range

7. A linear function has _____ variable(s).

8. $3x + 9 = y$ and $f(x) = 2 + 2x$ are both _____.

9. The set of all values of x is called the _____.

Determine whether each expression is a linear equation (E) or a linear function (F).

10. $6 - 3x = f(x)$ _____

11. $y = 4x + 2$ _____

12. $3x + y = 11$ _____

13. $f(x) = 2y + 5$ _____

14. $2y = 4x$ _____

15. $4y - 2 = f(x)$ _____

16. $7 = 1y + 2x$ _____

Unit 4, Lesson 1: Linear Functions, Linear Equations, and Systems of Linear Equations

Complete the following statements using words from the box.

1. $y = 12 - 2x$ would be classified as a(n) _____ equation.

2. Both linear functions and linear equations create a _____ when graphed.

3. _____ is a linear equation.

4. A system of linear equations has _____ variable(s).

5. A linear equation can be put in the form $ax + by = c$, where a, b, and c are numbers, and where a and b are not both _____.

6. A linear function has a _____ rate of change and can be modeled by a straight line.

7. A system of linear equations has more than one _____.

8. A _____ is a letter that represents an unknown number.

9. A function is a(n) _____ that assigns exactly one value from the range to the domain.

linear
one
$f(x) = 3x + 2$
equation
line
relationship
$y = x + 2$
different
systems
system of linear equations
matching
constant
circle
zero
variable

Determine whether each expression is a linear equation (E) or a linear function (F).

10. $f(x) = y + 9$

12. $2x + 7y = 15$

14. $6x - 3 = y$

16. $2x + 4y = 24$

_____   _____   _____   _____

11. $9x = y + 2$

13. $y - 4 = f(x)$

15. $6x - 3 = f(x)$

_____   _____   _____

Unit 4, Lesson 3: The Equation of a Line

Solve.

1. What is the formula for finding the slope of a line using the coordinates of two points on a line?
   _____

2. Using the graph on the right, write a fraction to show the difference in the y-coordinates over the difference in the x-coordinates. _____

3. Subtract the y-coordinates and the x-coordinates.
   _____

4. Simplify. What is the slope of the line?
   _____

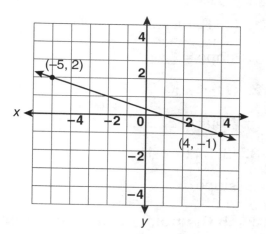

Find the slope of the line through each pair of points.

5. $(8, 2)$, $(4, 1)$

   _____

6. $(6, -2)$, $(4, 3)$

   _____

7. $(4, 1)$, $(-9, 1)$

   _____

8. $(-3, 6)$, $(5, -1)$

   _____

9. $(3, -1)$, $(5, 5)$

   _____

10. $(-2, -7)$, $(-2, 0)$

    _____

Find the slope of each line by choosing two points on the line whose coordinates are easy to read.

11. _____

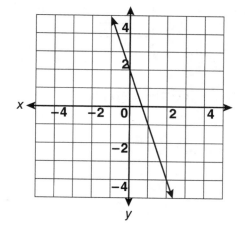

12. _____

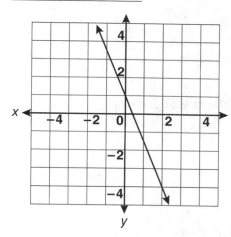

Name _____ Date _____

Unit 4, Lesson 3: The Equation of a Line

Find the slope of the line through each pair of points.

1. (4, 1), (0, −2)

slope = _____

2. (1, −1), (0, 0)

slope = _____

3. (2, 2), (0, −1)

slope = _____

4. (−1, −3), (5, 4)

slope = _____

5. (−1, 2), (4, −3)

slope = _____

6. (−2, 0), (0, 1)

slope = _____

Graph the points from questions 1–6 below. Next, write in *y*-intercept form, or *y* = *mx* + *b*, where *m* is the slope of the line and *b* is the *y*-intercept.

7. 1.

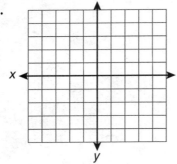

y-intercept form _____

9. 3.

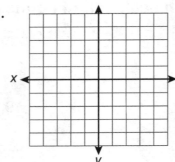

y-intercept form _____

11. 5.

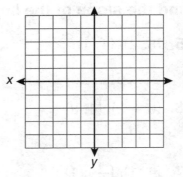

y-intercept form _____

8. 2.

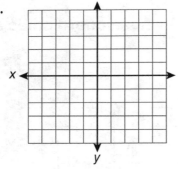

y-intercept form _____

10. 4.

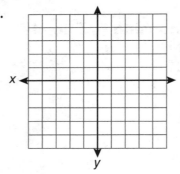

y-intercept form _____

12. 6.

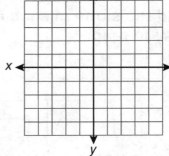

y-intercept form _____

Unit 4, Lesson 6: Using the x- and y-Intercepts to Graph a Linear Equation

Find the x-intercept and y-intercept. Next, use the intercepts to graph the equation.

1. $x + 5y = 10$

   x-intercept _____

   y-intercept _____

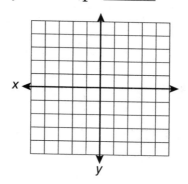

3. $x + 2y = 8$

   x-intercept _____

   y-intercept _____

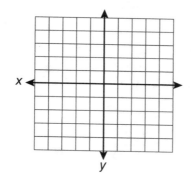

5. $-2x - 4y = 12$

   x-intercept _____

   y-intercept _____

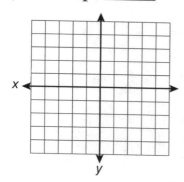

2. $2x + 3y = 6$

   x-intercept _____

   y-intercept _____

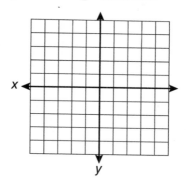

4. $x - 2y = -8$

   x-intercept _____

   y-intercept _____

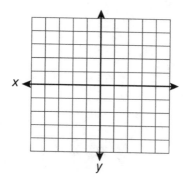

Name _____ Date _____

Unit 4, Lesson 6: Using the *x*- and *y*-Intercepts to Graph a Linear Equation

Find the x-intercept and y-intercept. Next, use the intercepts to graph the equation.

1. $-3x + 6y = -12$

x-intercept _____

y-intercept _____

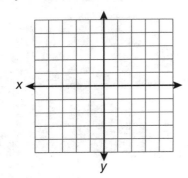

3. $7x - 2y = 14$

x-intercept _____

y-intercept _____

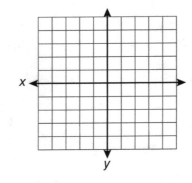

5. $2x - y = -2$

x-intercept _____

y-intercept _____

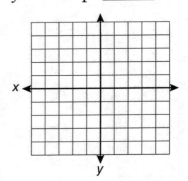

2. $3x - 3y = 9$

x-intercept _____

y-intercept _____

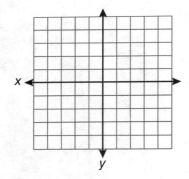

4. $-5x - 5y = 5$

x-intercept _____

y-intercept _____

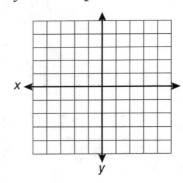

Name _____ Date _____

Unit 4, Lesson 9: Connections Between Nonlinear Equations and Their Graphs

Classify each of the following equations as linear (L) or nonlinear (N).

1. $x - y = -3$ _____

2. $y = -2 + 0x$ _____

3. $x + 4y = -16$ _____

4. $0 = 5y - x$ _____

5. $x = y^2$ _____

6. $y = x^2 + 6$ _____

7. $x - 2 = y$ _____

8. $6x - 3y = 9$ _____

9. $-16 = 8x - 2y$ _____

10. $x^2 = -1 + 4y$ _____

Match each problem with the correct answer. For the points, find which linear equation shows the line where they are found.

11. $y = 5x - 2$ _____   **A** $(2, 8)$

12. nonlinear equation _____   **B** $y = ax^2 + bx + c$

13. $y = 2x + 1$ _____   **C** $y = mx + b$

14. equation of a line _____   **D** $2x - 4y = 6$

15. $y = x - 5$ _____   **E** $y = x^2 + 6$

16. equation of a parabola _____   **F** $(3, 7)$

17. linear equation _____   **G** $(10, 5)$

18. $\dfrac{\text{change in } y}{\text{change in } x}$ _____   **H** slope of a line

Name _____ Date _____

Unit 4, Lesson 9: Connections Between Nonlinear Equations and Their Graphs

Fill in each table. Then graph the points below.

1. $y = x^2$

x	−3	−2	−1	0	1	2	3
y	9						

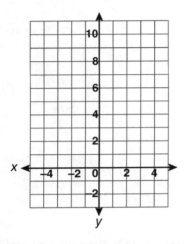

2. $y = 2x^2$

x	−3	−2	−1	0	1	2	3
y	18						

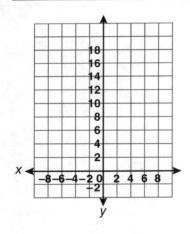

3. $y = -1x^2$

x	−3	−2	−1	0	1	2	3
y							

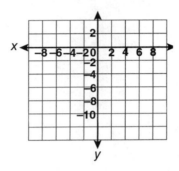

4. $y = (x^2 - 1) - 2$

x	−3	−2	−1	0	1	2	3
y							

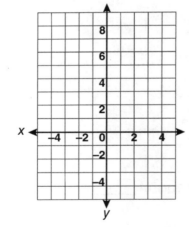

Name _____ Date _____

Unit 4, Lesson 11: Solving Systems of Linear Equations with Two Variables

Convert into slope-intercept form.

1. $-1 = -2x + y$

_____

2. $10 = 5y - x$

_____

3. $y + 4x = -1$

_____

4. $y + 2x = 3$

_____

5. $x - y = -4$

_____

6. $y - x = -1$

_____

7. $x + 6 + y = 0$

_____

8. $2x - 4y = 0$

_____

9. $-10 + 6y = -2x$

_____

10. $y - 1 = -4x$

_____

Next, find the slope of the line for questions 1–10.

11. 1. slope = _____
12. 2. slope = _____
13. 3. slope = _____
14. 4. slope = _____
15. 5. slope = _____

16. 6. slope = _____
17. 7. slope = _____
18. 8. slope = _____
19. 9. slope = _____
20. 10. slope = _____

Find ordered pairs using −1, 0, 1, and 2 for x.

21. $y = 5x$ _____
22. $y = -4x - 2$ _____
23. $y = -3x - 1$ _____
24. $y = x^2$ _____
25. $y = x + 2$ _____

26. $y = (3x + 1)^2$ _____
27. $y = 2x - 1$ _____
28. $y = \frac{1}{2}x + 1$ _____
29. $y = 3x - 4$ _____

Unit 4, Lesson 11: Solving Systems of Linear Equations with Two Variables

For each equation, solve for *y* by substituting the numbers given for *x*. Then graph the two equations using the ordered pairs you have found. The point of intersection is the solution to the system of equations.

1. $x = -1, 0, 1, 2$

$y = 5x + 1$

$y = x - 3$

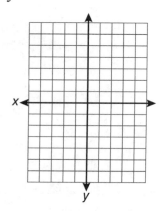

Solution _____

3. $x = -2, -1, 0, 1$

$y = x - 5$

$y = 4x + 1$

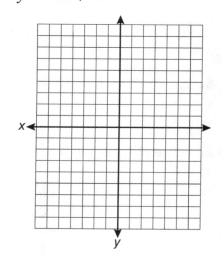

Solution _____

5. $x = 0, 1, 2, 3$

$y = 3x - 9$

$y = -x - 1$

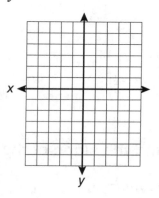

Solution _____

2. $x = -1, -\frac{1}{2}, 0, 1$

$y = 2x + 1$

$y = -2x - 1$

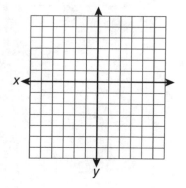

Solution _____

4. $x = -1, 0, 1, 2$

$y = x - 3$

$y = -x - 3$

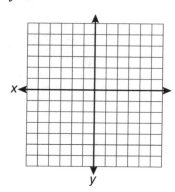

Solution _____

Unit 4, Lesson 13: Verbal, Algebraic, and Graphical Representations of Functions

Replace each verbal expression with its algebraic equivalent. Let x stand for "some number."

1. "some number squared"
_____

2. "y equals m times some number plus b" _____

3. "some number plus five equals four" _____

4. "f of x equals four plus the product of two and some number"
_____

5. "f of x equals fifteen plus three times some number" _____

6. "y equals two subtracted from one-third times some number"
_____

7. "square the product of five and two"
_____

8. "y equals negative four plus three times some number" _____

9. "y equals five subtracted from negative two-fifths" _____

10. "the sum of ten plus ten multiplied by some number" _____

11. "thirty-eight hundredths times three"
_____

12. "one and one-tenth subtracted from thirteen and two-tenths" _____

13. "negative four plus negative one"
_____

14. "negative two plus nine times some number" _____

15. "the difference of negative two and five multiplied by b" _____

16. "the sum of negative two and three times some number equals negative seventeen"
_____

17. "the sum of negative one-third times some number and eight equals f of x"
_____

18. "some number times the quotient of fifty-four divided by nine"
_____

19. "from seventy-one thousand, three hundred eleven subtract three thousand, nine hundred eighty-three" _____

Unit 4, Lesson 13: Verbal, Algebraic, and Graphical Representations of Functions

Replace each verbal function with its algebraic equivalent. Let x stand for "some number."

1. "*f* of *x* equals nine multiplied by some number subtracted from twenty-seven" _____

2. "negative seven times some number subtracted from some number equals *f* of *x*" _____

3. "the sum of three and four-tenths, three and four hundredths, and some number equals *f* of *x*" _____

4. "*f* of *x* equals the quotient of negative three and some number squared" _____

5. "ten subtracted from one-half of *x* plus two times some number equals *f* of *x*" _____

6. "the sum of three and the product of four and some number equals *f* of *x*" _____

7. "thirty-six hundredths subtracted from twenty-four and six-tenths times some number equals *f* of *x*" _____

8. "*f* of *x* equals the difference of sixty-five and some number squared" _____

9. "seven subtracted from some number times twenty equals *f* of *x*" _____

10. "twelve plus five times some number equals *f* of *x*" _____

11. "*f* of *x* equals the sum of some number and three squared" _____

12. "two to the third power times the quotient of five and some number equals *f* of *x*" _____

13. "*f* of *x* equals eleven to the fourth power times seven plus some number" _____

14. "*f* of *x* equals one-fifth times some number plus eight-tenths" _____

15. "*f* of *x* equals the product of negative two plus sixteen and some number" _____

16. "four times some number subtracted from negative three times some number equals *f* of *x*" _____

17. "*f* of *x* equals twenty-one times some number subtracted from thirty-four" _____

18. "*f* of *x* equals the difference of nineteen times some number and three squared" _____

19. "the product of nine plus four and some number equals *f* of *x*" _____

20. "the product of two times some number and five equals *f* of *x*" _____

Unit 4, Lesson 16: Using Linear Equations, Linear Functions, and Systems of Linear Equations to Solve Problems

Solve by isolating y on the left side of the equation.

1. $3x + y = 6$

_____

2. $5x + 20 + y = 0$

_____

3. $x + y = -4$

_____

4. $6x + 3y = 9$

_____

5. $4x - 2y = 8$

_____

Solve the system of equations. Give the ordered pair of (x, y).

6. $2x - y = 6$

$-x + y = -1$

_____

7. $3x + 3y = -6$

$-2x + 2y = 8$

_____

8. $2x + 7y = -1$

$-x - 2y = 2$

_____

9. $3x - y = 2$

$x + y = 2$

_____

10. $x - 3y = -33$

$2x + 3y = 6$

_____

11. $3x - 2y = 4$

$y = 3 - x$

_____

Unit 4, Lesson 16: Using Linear Equations, Linear Functions, and Systems of Linear Equations to Solve Problems

Solve by isolating y on the left side of the equation.

1. $2y + 1x = 1$

_____

2. $-x + 5 + y = 3$

_____

3. $-4 = 1x - 1y$

_____

4. $-x + y = -9$

_____

5. $y - 4 = 3x$

_____

Solve the system of equations. Give the ordered pair of (x, y).

6. $y = 3x - 4$

$7x - 5y = 4$

_____

7. $x + y = 4$

$3x + 4y = 10$

_____

8. $3x - 4y = 2$

$5x + 2y = 12$

_____

9. $2y - 5x = -1$

$x = 2y + 5$

_____

10. $x + 4y = 7$

$3x + 7y = 6$

_____

11. $6x - 2y = 4$

$y = 6 - x$

_____

Name _____ Date _____

Unit 4, Lesson 19:
Arithmetic Sequences as Linear Functions

Find the next three numbers in each sequence.

1. 2, 5, 8, 11, _____, _____, _____

2. 3, 6, 12, 24, _____, _____, _____

3. 9, 18, 27, 36, _____, _____, _____

4. 64, 56, 48, 40, _____, _____, _____

5. 1, 4, 16, 64, _____, _____, _____

6. 75, 70, 65, 60, _____, _____, _____

7. 90, 81, 72, 63, _____, _____, _____

8. 4, 8, 16, 32, _____, _____, _____

9. 4, 7, 10, 13, _____, _____, _____

10. 12, 14, 17, 21, _____, _____, _____

11. 19, 29, 39, 49, _____, _____, _____

12. 128, 64, 32, 16, _____, _____, _____

13. 135, 125, 115, 105, _____, _____, _____

14. 5, 10, 20, 40, _____, _____, _____

Solve.

15. Write the first five terms in a number pattern starting with
the number 6. Next, write the rule that describes your pattern.

_____

_____

_____

Name _____   Date _____

Unit 4, Lesson 19:
Arithmetic Sequences as Linear Functions

Find the missing number in each sequence.

1. 7, 21, 63, _____, 567

2. 33, 27, _____, 15, 9

3. 14, 23, 32, _____, 50

4. _____, 20, 80, 320, 1,280

5. 3, 9, 27, _____, 243

6. 1, 8, 15, 22, _____

7. 48, 24, 12, _____, 3

Sketch the next two designs in each pattern.

8.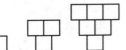

9.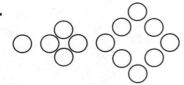

10. ♥♥♥♥♥♥   ♥♥♥♥♥
     ♥♥♥♥♥♥   ♥♥♥♥
     ♥♥♥♥♥♥   ♥♥♥♥
     ♥♥♥♥♥♥

11. ▲ ▲   ▲ ▲
     ▲ ▲   ▲ ▲
     ▲ ▲   ▲ ▲
     ▲ ▲

Solve.

12. Start with the arithmetic sequence 7, 9, 11, 13,…

A Make a table where the x-value is the number of the term and the y-value is the term.

x	y
1	7
2	9
3	11
4	13
5	?

B What is the equation of the arithmetic sequence 7, 9, 11, 13, …?

_____

C Using the table, what would the coordinates be if you were to graph this equation?

_____

D Remember, to find the slope of a line find the difference in y over the difference in x.

What is the slope of the line?

$$m = \frac{y_2 - y_1}{x_2 - x_1} = \frac{(9 - 7)}{(\underline{\quad} - \underline{\quad})} = \underline{\quad}$$

Answer Key

Unit 2, Lesson 1, Page 5

1. 6
2. 56
3. 4
4. 1
5. 8
6. 9
7. 48
8. 40
9. 12
10. 3
11. 7
12. 16
13. 24
14. 15
15. 36
16. 4
17. 2
18. 18
19. 6
20. 20
21. 15 newspapers
22. 6 movies
23. 2:1
24. 12 marbles

Unit 2, Lesson 1, Page 6

1. 1
2. 50
3. 20
4. 25
5. 10
6. 12
7. 10
8. 27
9. 11
10. 9
11. 88 laps
12. 7:15

Unit 2, Lesson 3, Page 7

1. 3
2. 32
3. 9
4. 12.6
5. 108
6. 455
7. 21
8. 50.4
9. 30
10. 40.5
11. 11.28
12. 7.8
13. 29.6
14. 4
15. 504
16. 684
17. 137.5
18. 75.6
19. 46.2
20. 212
21. 12 gallons
22. 24 games
23. $162
24. Number of Students: Babysitting: 308; Sports: 364; Job: 210; At home: 140; Tutoring: 140; Other: 238

Unit 2, Lesson 3, Page 8

1. 25
2. 49
3. 7
4. 30
5. 40
6. 7.2
7. 19.2
8. 40.5
9. 43.2
10. 66
11. 171
12. 12.8
13. 30%
14. 10%
15. Square Roots
16. B 45%
17. D 55.2

Unit 2, Lesson 6, Page 9

1. $1.08; $16.92
2. $46.86; $166.14
3. $14.40; $65.60
4. $11.16; $112.84
5. $282.24; $389.76
6. $13.68
7. $13.90
8. yes
9. $126
10. $2.40

Unit 2, Lesson 6, Page 10

1. $9
2. $14.40
3. $18
4. $1.80
5. $4.80
6. $42
7. $3
8. $13,375
9. $12,973.75
10. $129.60

Unit 2, Lesson 9, Page 11

1. 60 channels
2. 18 shows
3. 120 times
4. 72 times
5. 48 times
6. $x = 6$
7. $x = 18.75$
8. $x = 54$
9. $x = 70$
10. $x = 15.5$

Unit 2, Lesson 9, Page 12

1. 40 times
2. 36 times
3. 9 times
4. 18 times
5. 16 fives
6. 55%
7. 32.5%
8. $x = 4$
9. $x = 10$
10. $x = 24$

Unit 2, Lesson 11, Page 13

1. 2:7
2. 1:5
3. 1:3
4. 1:2
5. 3:8
6. 4:11
7. 5:9
8. 1:4

Unit 2, Lesson 11, Page 14

1. yes
2. no
3. yes
4. no
5. 10
6. 2.25
7. 33
8. 22.5

Unit 2, Lesson 13, Page 15

1. $1.83 per slice
2. $0.40 per bottle
3. 4.15 miles per hour
4. $0.15 per egg
5. $8.75 per shirt
6. $10.75 per hour
7. 3.25 miles per hour
8. $0.10 per text message
9. $0.63 per pound
10. 55 miles per hour
11. 3
12. $\frac{5}{4}$
13. $\frac{2}{9}$
14. $\frac{1}{8}$
15. $\frac{1}{9}$

Unit 2, Lesson 13, Page 16

See student graph for questions 1–6.

Unit 2, Lesson 16, Page 17

1. 198.66
2. 40%
3. 2.4%
4. 7.7
5. 21.25
6. 910
7. 72.5%
8. 360
9. 1.2
10. 45.45
11. circle graph
12. histogram
13. histogram
14. circle graph
15. circle graph

Unit 2, Lesson 16, Page 18

1. 30 people
2. 60 people
3. 110 people
4. 240 people
5. 10 people
6. 60%
7. 96%
8. about 9%
9. about 71%
10. about 29%
11. 48%
12. about 3%

Unit 2, Lesson 19, Page 19

1. 150 people
2. 8 people
3. 3 people
4. 252 people
5. 900 people
6. 520 people
7. 400 people
8. 60 people
9. 9,600 people
10. 5 people
11. 75 people
12. 500 households

Unit 2, Lesson 19, Page 20

1. 1,400 people
2. 800 people; 1,200 people
3. 200 people
4. 24,000 people
5. 160 people

Unit 3, Lesson 1, Page 21

1. 56
2. 14
3. 4,312
4. 218
5. 111
6. 3,529
7. 5
8. 78
9. 1
10. −756
11. −9,023
12. 61
13. 26
14. −813
15. <
16. <
17. >
18. >
19. >
20. <

Unit 3, Lesson 1, Page 22

1. 18, 4, −1, −9, −22
2. 10, 1, 0, −1, −5
3. 3, −10, −11, −32, −64
4. 82, 19, 0, −2, −19
5. 12, 1, −6, −77, −100

For questions 6–10, answers will vary. One example is given for each question.

6. 4.6
7. $6\frac{3}{4}$
8. $9\frac{1}{2}$
9. 16.9
10. $\frac{8}{8} = 1$
11. −3
12. 12
13. −187
14. −56
15. 8
16. 24

Unit 3, Lesson 3, Page 23

1. 29
2. −85
3. −37
4. 137
5. 207
6. −51
7. 0
8. −59
9. −328
10. 4
11. −33
12. 0
13. −63
14. −101
15. −114
16. E −35
17. B 0
18. C −122
19. A 407
20. D −7

Unit 3, Lesson 3, Page 24

1. 512
2. −105
3. −7

4.

![number line 4] 3

$-3\ -2\ -1\ 0\ 1\ 2\ 3\ 4\ 5\ 6$

5.

![number line 5] -9

$-9\ -8\ -7\ -6\ -5\ -4\ -3\ -2\ -1\ 0\ 1\ 2$

6.

![number line 6] -5

$-5\ -4\ -3\ -2\ -1\ 0\ 1\ 2\ 3\ 4\ 5$

7.

![number line 7] 2

$-5\ -4\ -3\ -2\ -1\ 0\ 1\ 2\ 3\ 4\ 5$

8.

![number line 8] -9

$-10\ -9\ -8\ -7\ -6\ -5\ -4\ -3\ -2\ -1\ 0\ 1$

9. 110
10. -60
11. -3
12. $16

Unit 3, Lesson 6, Page 25

1. -112
2. 55
3. 5
4. -43
5. 22
6. -14
7. -184
8. 124
9. -828
10. 188
11. -16
12. $-2{,}022$
13. -155
14. 336

Unit 3, Lesson 6, Page 26

1. E -37
2. I 693
3. L -595
4. A -21
5. C -130
6. K -213
7. D 2
8. H -468
9. positive
10. 22
11. negative
12. -154

Unit 3, Lesson 9, Page 27

1. $x = \frac{10}{3}$ or $3\frac{1}{3}$
2. $x = \frac{8}{27}$
3. $x = \frac{9}{11}$
4. $x = \frac{2}{3}$
5. $x = \frac{35}{8}$ or $4\frac{3}{8}$
6. $x = \frac{56}{45}$ or $1\frac{11}{45}$
7. $x = \frac{94}{45}$ or $2\frac{4}{45}$
8. $x = \frac{119}{25}$ or $4\frac{19}{25}$
9. $x = \frac{5}{3}$ or $1\frac{2}{3}$
10. $x = \frac{3}{4}$
11. $x = \frac{5}{4}$ or $1\frac{1}{4}$
12. $x = \frac{20}{9}$ or $2\frac{2}{9}$
13. $x = \frac{3}{5}$
14. $x = 6$

Unit 3, Lesson 9, Page 28

1. $\frac{12}{11}$ or $1\frac{1}{11}$
2. $\frac{35}{24}$ or $1\frac{11}{24}$
3. $\frac{16}{21}$
4. $\frac{38}{15}$ or $2\frac{8}{15}$
5. $\frac{13}{18}$
6. $\frac{9}{11}$
7. $\frac{32}{27}$ or $1\frac{5}{27}$
8. $\frac{7}{20}$
9. $\frac{3}{4}$
10. $\frac{459}{50}$ or $9\frac{9}{50}$
11. $\frac{45}{4}$ or $11\frac{1}{4}$
12. $\frac{7}{15}$

Unit 3, Lesson 11, Page 29

1. $m - 8 = 74$
2. $2n - 4$
3. $t = \frac{c}{2}$ or $\frac{1}{2}c$
4. $4r = 56$
5. $532 - d = 224$
6. $12s = 48$
7. $12j$
8. $8 + f = 17$

9. $600 - t = 180$
10. $12 - 4 = w$
11. $15 + s = 23$
12. $8t$

Unit 3, Lesson 11, Page 30

1. $j + 6 - 9$
2. $400 \times f$
3. $96 - c$
4. $\frac{52}{x}$
5. $h \times 84$
6. $k + 10 + 1$
7. $\$350 - n$
8. $200 \div n$
9. $30n$
10. $40 - n$
11. $n - 2$
12. $n + 3$

Unit 3, Lesson 13, Page 31

1. $j = 9$
2. $y = 123$
3. $s = -8$
4. $z = 19$
5. $m = -5$
6. $n = 200$
7. $g = -48$
8. $p = 99$
9. $c = 0$
10. $k = 3$
11. $t = 115$
12. $g = 68$
13. $h = 87$
14. $x = -42$
15. $x = 26$
16. $b = 12$
17. $e = 210$
18. $d = 80$
19. $r = 8$
20. $z = -16$

Unit 3, Lesson 13, Page 32

1. 35 dishes
2. 16 minutes
3. 15 horses
4. $32
5. $36
6. 14 pounds
7. 7 hours
8. 13 blankets
9. C $p = 13$
10. F $p = 15$
11. B $p = 24$
12. A $p = 85$
13. D $p = 77$
14. E $p = 72$

Unit 3, Lesson 16, Page 33

1. yes
2. no
3. yes
4. yes
5. yes
6. no
7. $x = 8$
8. $s = 13$
9. $d = 64$
10. $m = 53$
11. $e = 147$
12. $c = -120$

Unit 3, Lesson 16, Page 34

1. yes
2. no
3. yes
4. yes
5. no
6. D not equivalent
7. B both
8. A equivalent
9. $x = 12$
10. $p = 614$
11. $n = 4$
12. $g = 21$

Unit 3, Lesson 19, Page 35

1. 72
  8   9
2 4   3 3
  2 2
$2^3 \times 3^2$

2. 84
  4   21
2 2   3 7
$2^2 \times 3 \times 7$

3. $2^2 \times 3$
4. $2^2 \times 3^2$
5. $2^2 \times 5$
6. 3×7
7. $2 \times 3^2 \times 5 \times 7$
8. $2^4 \times 5^2$
9. $2^3 \times 5$
10. $2^2 \times 3 \times 5$
11. $2 \times 3 \times 5$
12. 2×3^2
13. $2^2 \times 5^2$
14. $2^4 \times 5^3$
15. 2^6
16. $2^4 \times 5 \times 7$

Unit 3, Lesson 19, Page 36

1. 27,000
2. No, because 4 and 9 are not prime.
3. 56
4. No, 4 is not prime. It should be broken down down into 2^2.
5. A $2^4 \times 3$
6. I 53
7. $3^2 \times 5$
8. $3^2 \times 2^2$
9. $2 \times 3 \times 7$
10. prime
11. 2^4
12. 5×7
13. 2×3^2
14. prime

Unit 4, Lesson 1, Page 37

1. two
2. functions
3. range
4. straight
5. $f(x)$
6. system of linear equations
7. one
8. expressions
9. domain
10. F
11. E
12. E
13. F
14. E
15. F
16. E

Unit 4, Lesson 1, Page 38

1. linear
2. line
3. $y = x + 2$
4. matching
5. zero
6. constant
7. equation
8. variable
9. relationship
10. F
11. E
12. E
13. F
14. E
15. F
16. E

Unit 4, Lesson 3, Page 39

1. $m = \frac{y_1 - y_2}{x_1 - x_2}$
2. $m = \frac{2 - (-1)}{-5 - 4}$
3. $-\frac{3}{9}$
4. $-\frac{1}{3}$
5. $\frac{1}{4}$
6. $-\frac{5}{2}$
7. $\frac{0}{13}$ or 0
8. $-\frac{7}{8}$
9. 3
10. $-\frac{7}{0}$ or undefined
11. -3
12. $-\frac{5}{2}$

Unit 4, Lesson 3, Page 40

1. $\frac{3}{4}$
2. -1
3. $\frac{3}{2}$
4. $\frac{7}{6}$
5. -1
6. $\frac{1}{2}$

7.

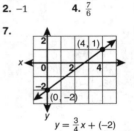

$y = \frac{3}{4}x + (-2)$

8.

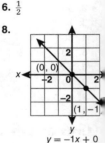

$y = -1x + 0$

9.

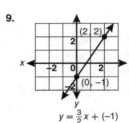

$y = \frac{3}{2}x + (-1)$

10.

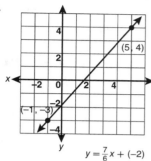

$y = \frac{7}{6}x + (-2)$

11.

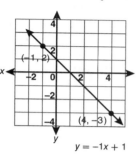

$y = -1x + 1$

12.

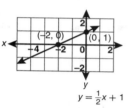

$y = \frac{1}{2}x + 1$

Unit 4, Lesson 6, Page 41

1. x-intercept $= (10, 0)$, y-intercept $= (0, 2)$

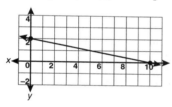

2. x-intercept $= (3, 0)$, y-intercept $= (0, 2)$

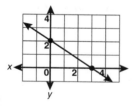

3. x-intercept $= (8, 0)$, y-intercept $= (0, 4)$

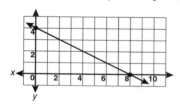

4. x-intercept $= (-8, 0)$, y-intercept $= (0, 4)$

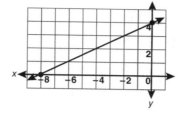

5. x-intercept $= (-6, 0)$, y-intercept $= (0, -3)$

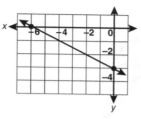

Unit 4, Lesson 6, Page 42

1. x-intercept $= (4, 0)$, y-intercept $= (0, -2)$

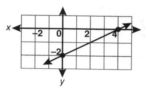

2. x-intercept $= (3, 0)$, y-intercept $= (0, -3)$

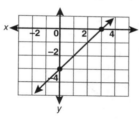

3. x-intercept $= (2, 0)$, **4.** x-intercept $= (-1, 0)$,
   y-intercept $= (-7, 0)$ y-intercept $= (0, -1)$

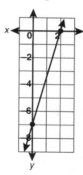

5. x-intercept $= (-1, 0)$, y-intercept $= (0, 2)$

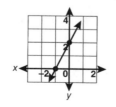

Unit 4, Lesson 9, Page 43

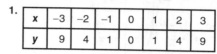

1. L	**7.** L	**13.** F
2. L	**8.** L	**14.** C
3. L	**9.** L	**15.** G
4. L	**10.** N	**16.** B
5. N	**11.** A	**17.** D
6. N	**12.** E	**18.** H

Unit 4, Lesson 9, Page 44

1.

x	−3	−2	−1	0	1	2	3
y	9	4	1	0	1	4	9

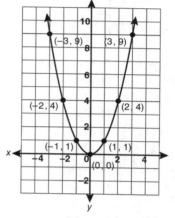

2.

x	−3	−2	−1	0	1	2	3
y	18	8	2	0	2	8	18

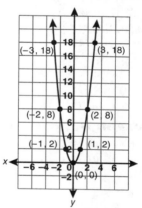

3.

x	−3	−2	−1	0	1	2	3
y	−9	−4	−1	0	−1	−4	−9

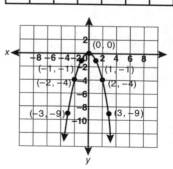

4.

x	−3	−2	−1	0	1	2	3
y	6	1	−2	−3	−2	1	6

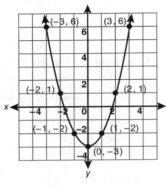

Unit 4, Lesson 11, Page 45

1. $y = 2x - 1$
2. $y = \frac{1}{5}x + 2$
3. $y = -4x - 1$
4. $y = -2x + 3$
5. $y = x + 4$
6. $y = x - 1$
7. $y = -x - 6$
8. $y = \frac{1}{2}x$
9. $y = -\frac{1}{3}x + \frac{5}{3}$
10. $y = -4x + 1$

11. slope $= 2$
12. slope $= \frac{1}{5}$
13. slope $= -4$
14. slope $= -2$
15. slope $= 1$
16. slope $= 1$
17. slope $= -1$
18. slope $= \frac{1}{2}$
19. slope $= -\frac{1}{3}$
20. slope $= -4$

21. (−1, −5), (0, 0), (1, 5), (2, 10)
22. (−1, 2), (0, −2), (1, −6), (2, −10)
23. (−1, 2), (0, −1), (1, −4), (2, −7)
24. (−1, 1), (0, 0), (1, 1), (2, 4)
25. (−1, 1), (0, 2), (1, 3), (2, 4)
26. (−1, 4), (0, 1), (1, 16), (2, 49)
27. (−1, −3), (0, −1), (1, 1), (2, 3)
28. (−1, $\frac{1}{2}$), (0, 1), (1, $\frac{3}{2}$), (2, 2)
29. (−1, −7), (0, −4), (1, −1), (2, 2)

Unit 4, Lesson 11, Page 46

1. $y = 5x + 1$: (−1, −4), (0, 1), (1, 6) (2, 11);
$y = x - 3$: (−1, −4), (0, −3) (1, −2), (2, −1)
Solution: (−1, −4)

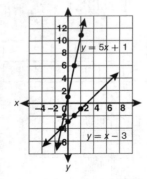

2. $y = 2x + 1$: (−1, −1), (−$\frac{1}{2}$, 0), (0, 1), (1, 3);
$y = -2x - 1$: (−1, 1), (−$\frac{1}{2}$, 0), (0, −1), (1, −3)
Solution: (−$\frac{1}{2}$, 0)

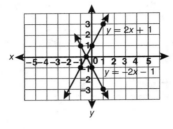

3. $y = x - 5$: (−2, −7), (−1, −6), (0, −5), (1, −4);
$y = 4x + 1$: (−2, −7) (−1, −3), (0, 1) (1, 5)
Solution: (−2, −7)

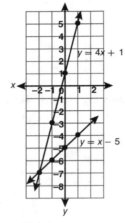

4. $y = x - 3$: (−1, −4), (0, −3), (1, −2); (2, −1);
$y = -x - 3$: (−1, −2), (0, −3), (1, −4), (2, −5)
Solution: (0, −3)

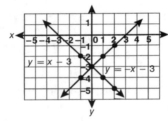

5. $y = 3x - 9$: (0, −9), (1, −6), (2, −3) (3, 0);
$y = -x - 1$: (0, −1), (1, −2), (2, −3), (3, −4)
Solution: (2, −3)

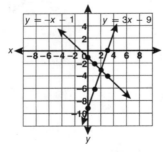

Unit 4, Lesson 13, Page 47

1. x^2
2. $y = mx + b$
3. $x + 5 = 4$
4. $f(x) = 4 + 2x$
5. $f(x) = 15 + 3x$
6. $y = \frac{1}{3}x - 2$
7. $(5 \times 2)^2$
8. $y = -4 + 3x$
9. $y = -\frac{2}{5} - 5$
10. $(10 + 10)x$
11. 0.38×3; $(\frac{38}{100})(3)$
12. $13\frac{2}{10} - 1\frac{1}{10}$; 13.2 − 1.1
13. $-4 + (-1)$

14. $-2 + 9x$
15. $(-2 - 5)b$
16. $(-2 + 3)x = -17$
17. $-\frac{1}{3}x + 8 = f(x)$
18. $(\frac{54}{9})x$
19. $71,311 - 3,983$

Unit 4, Lesson 13, Page 48

1. $f(x) = 27 - 9x$
2. $x - (-7x) = f(x)$
3. $3.4 + 3.04 + x = f(x)$
4. $f(x) = -(\frac{3}{x})^2$
5. $\frac{1}{2}x - 10 + 2x = f(x)$
6. $3 + 4x = f(x)$
7. $24.6x - 0.36 = f(x)$
8. $f(x) = 65 - x^2$
9. $20x - 7 = f(x)$
10. $12 + 5x = f(x)$

11. $f(x) = (x + 3)^2$
12. $(2^3)(\frac{5}{x}) = f(x)$
13. $f(x) = (11^4)(7 + x)$
14. $f(x) = \frac{1}{5}x + 0.8$
15. $f(x) = (-2 + 16)x$
16. $-3x - 4x = f(x)$
17. $f(x) = 34 - 21x$
18. $f(x) = 19x - 3^2$
19. $x(9 + 4) = f(x)$
20. $(2x)(5) = f(x)$

Unit 4, Lesson 16, Page 49

1. $y = 6 - 3x$
2. $y = -20 - 5x$
3. $y = -4 - x$
4. $y = 3 - 2x$
5. $y = -4 + 2x$
6. (5, 4)
7. (−3, 1)
8. (−4, 1)
9. (1, 1)
10. (−9, 8)
11. (2, 1)

Unit 4, Lesson 16, Page 50

1. $y = \frac{1}{2} - \frac{x}{2}$
2. $y = x - 2$
3. $y = 4 + x$
4. $y = -9 + x$
5. $y = 3x + 4$
6. (2, 2)
7. (6, −2)
8. (2, 1)
9. (−1, −3)
10. (−5, 3)
11. (2, 4)

Unit 4, Lesson 19, Page 51

1. 14, 17, 20
2. 48, 96, 192
3. 45, 54, 63
4. 32, 24, 16
5. 256; 1,024; 4,096
6. 55, 50, 45
7. 54, 45, 36
8. 64, 128, 256
9. 16, 19, 22
10. 26, 32, 39
11. 59, 69, 79
12. 8, 4, 2
13. 95, 85, 75
14. 80, 160, 320
15. Answers will vary.

Unit 4, Lesson 19, Page 52

1. 189
2. 21
3. 41
4. 5
5. 81
6. 29
7. 6

8. 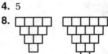 9.

10. ♥♥ ♥
♥♥ ♥
♥♥ ♥

11. ▲▲ ▲▲
▲▲

12. A

x	y
1	7
2	9
3	11
4	13
5	15

B $y = 2x + 5$
C (1, 7), (2, 9), (3, 11), (4, 13), (5, 15)
D 2 − 1, 2